£3.95

Printed and Published in Great Britain by D. C. THOMSON & CO., LTD., 185 Fleet Street, London EC4A 2HS.

© D. C. THOMSON & CO., LTD., 1992.
ISBN 0-85116-542-7.

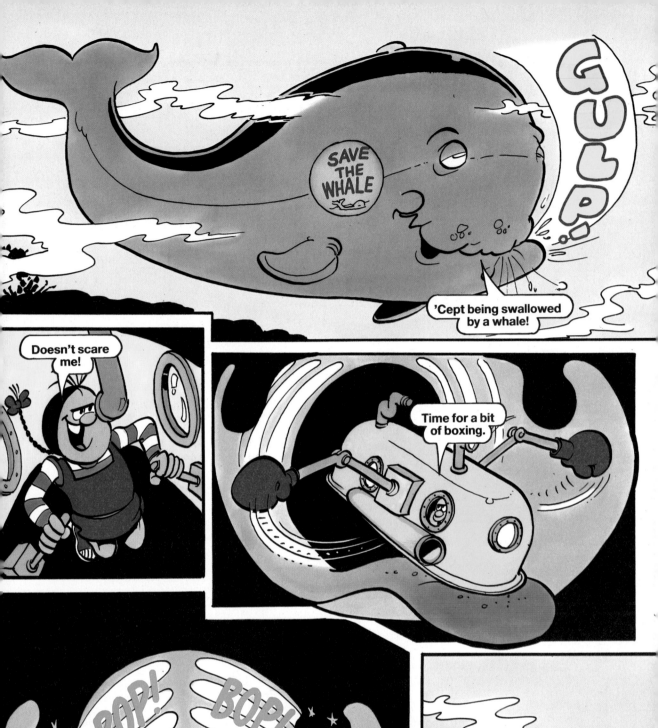

TRICKY DICKY

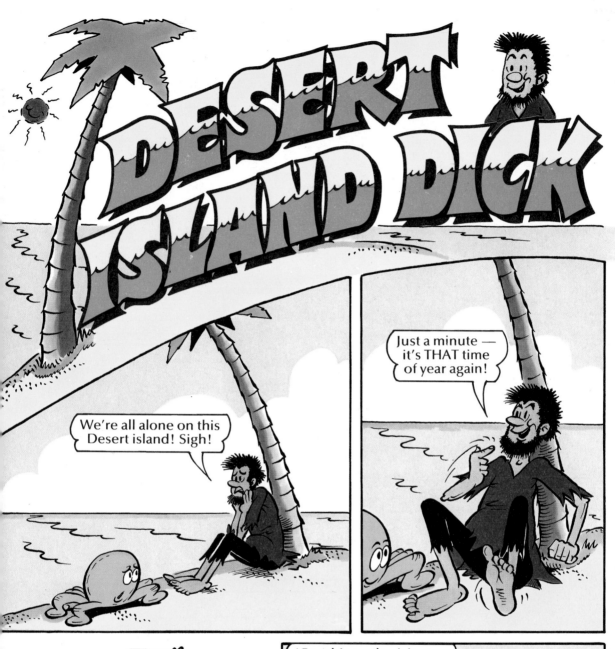

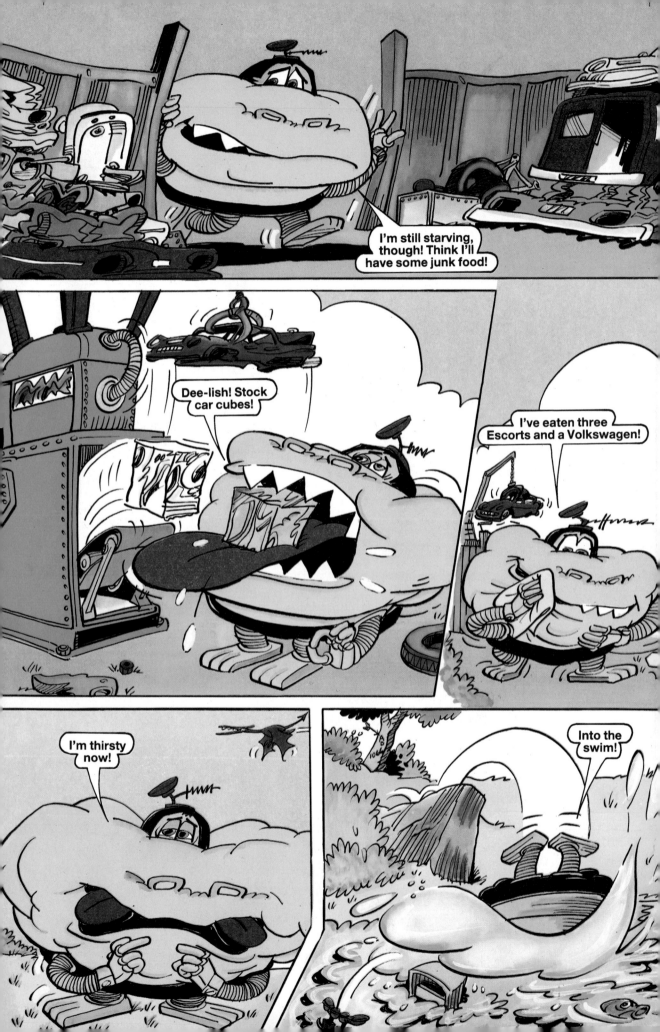

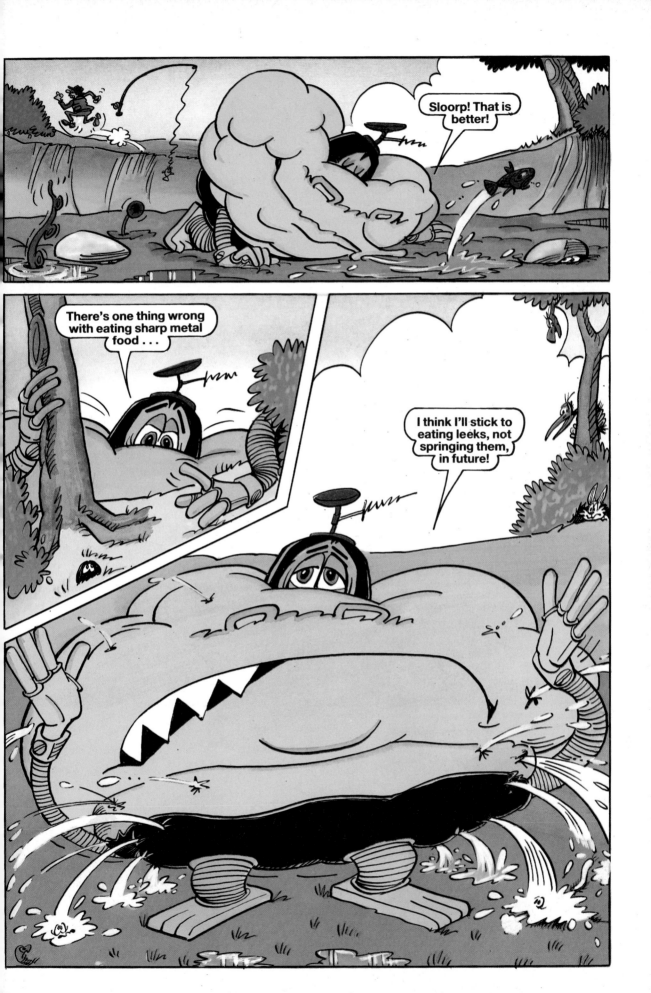

PXQZTKLE

Class, this is Roger, our new pupil. He's very homesick, so be nice to him!

Waah! I hate it here! My old school was so much nicer! Boo-hoo!

This isn't such a bad school, Roger! You'l get used to it — just like I did.

You're lucky here — imagine if the teachers were from Sirius A, for instance!

Look, I'll show you —

A d-dog!

Well Sirius IS the DOG STAR!

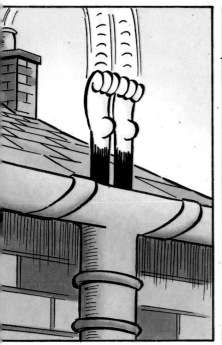

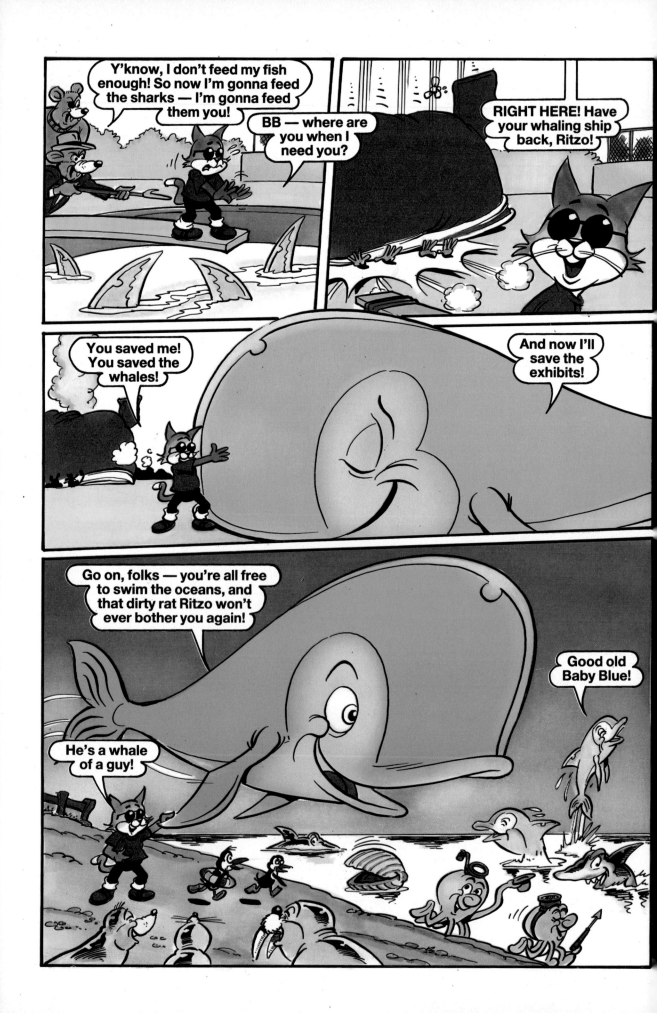

RED MIST
WHAT ARE YOU LOOKING AT, MATE?

I hate Saturdays! Why does everybody go shopping on Saturdays?

But you're going shopping too!

And there's always some idiot blocking the street! Out of the way!

I'm a failure — he didn't smile!

He NEVER smiles!

Expensive little lot!

Can I help you, Sir?

No! I don't want any help!

You can't even LOOK these days without somebody trying to hassle you into buying!

Hey! I like that!

Where's the assistant?

Why is there NEVER an assistant around when you want one? Snarl!

I hate Saturdays! Why can't you stupid lot shop on a Monday? You're all in my way!

Rant! Rave!

You, young man, are blocking the street!

Roll on Sunday!

TRICKY DICKY'S TOY CUPBOARD

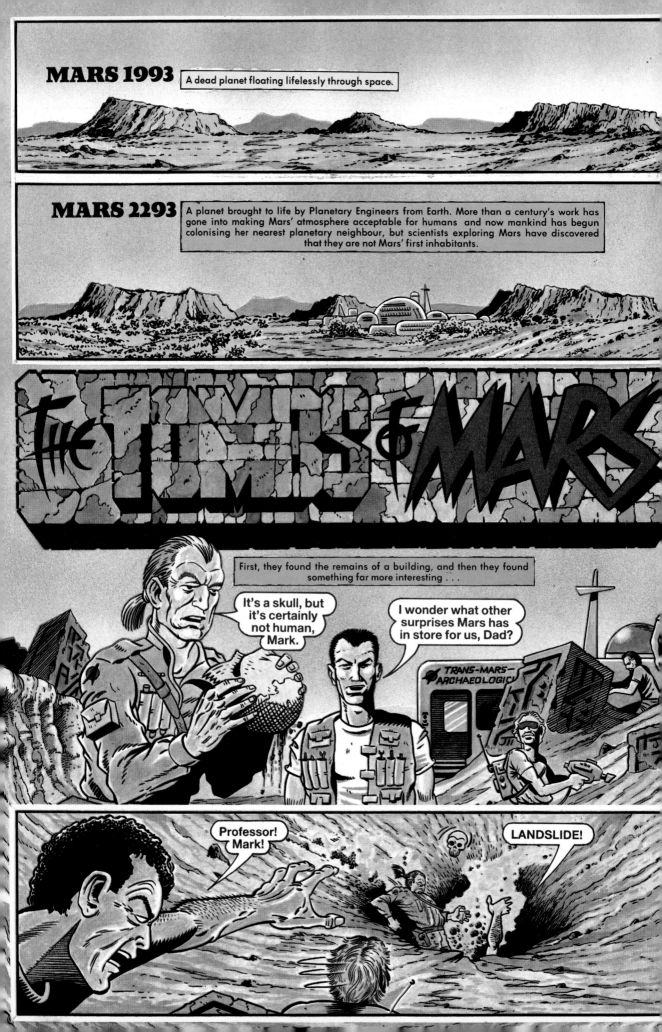

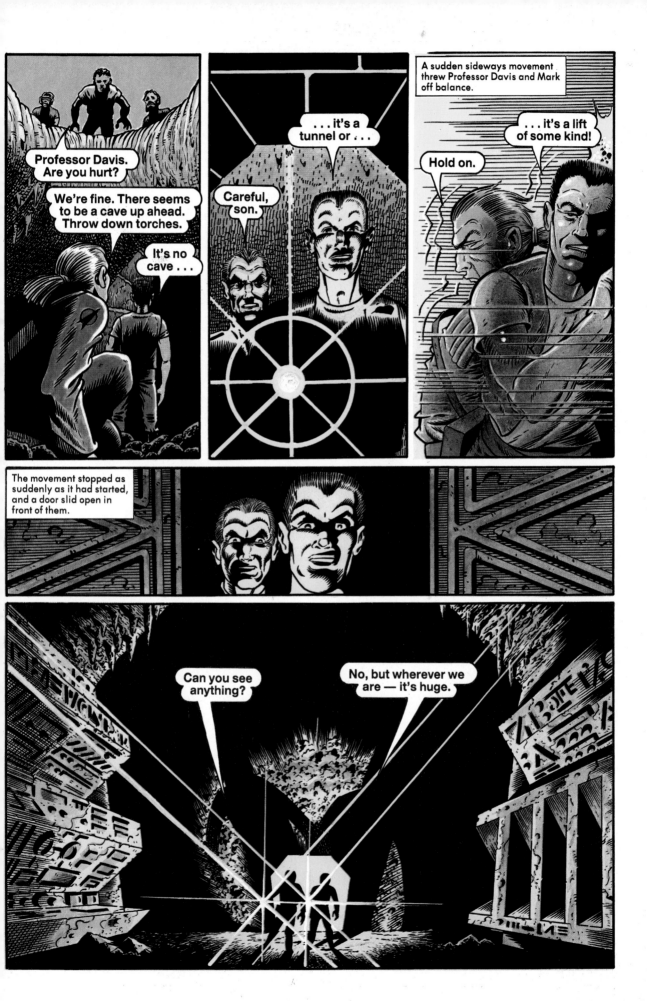

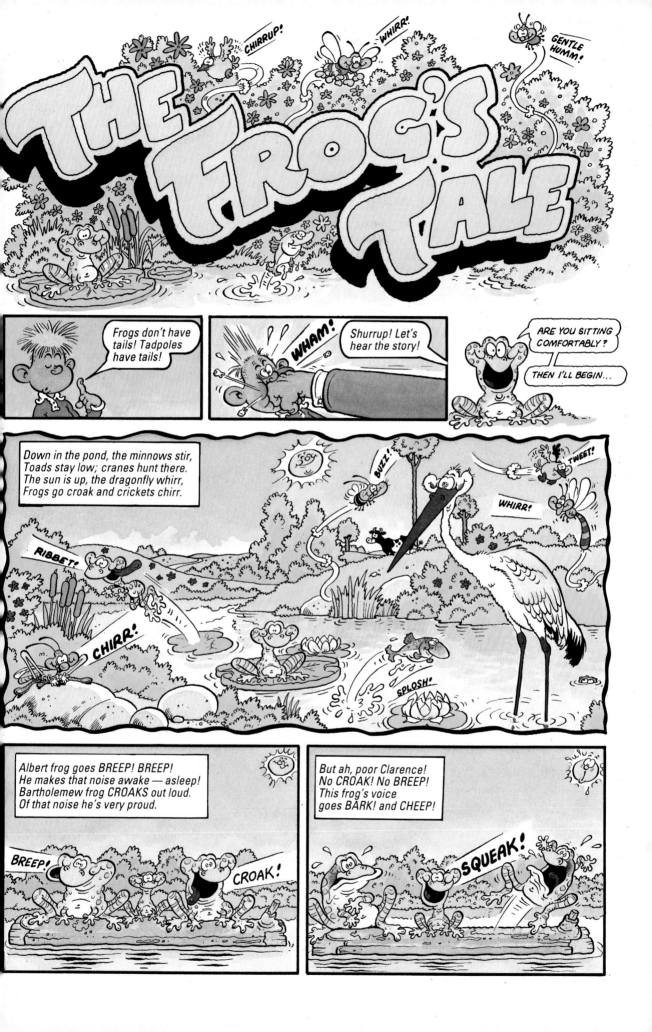

It's a problem,
as you can tell.
A frog that MOOS!
And CUCKOOS! as well!

MEOW!

He puffs his chest!
He goes for broke!
Despite these tries—
Clarence can't CROAK!

HEE-HAW!

Some frogs RIBBET!
Some go BRRRUCK!
But our poor Clarence—
no such luck!

Frogs eat worms,
grubs and flies.
Perhaps that causes
their distinctive cries.

But a friend suggests
a change of diet.
Our Clarence thinks,
"May as well try it!"

CHOMP!
NOSH!

CHEW!

SHLUPP!

So he started eating
trout and crane.
Soon he moved up
the food chain.

He ate some sheep,
the occasional bull.
His belly expanded—
he got so full!

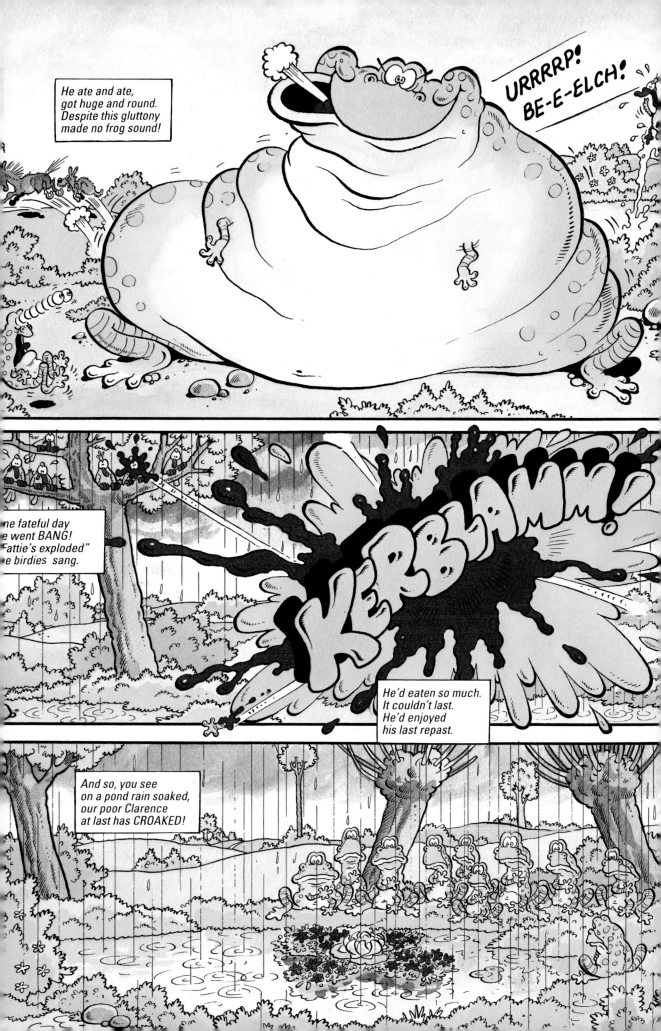